C000185714

BRITAIN IN OLD P

LEICESTERSHIRE AT WAR

ROBIN P. JENKINS

SUTTON PUBLISHING LIMITED

Sutton Publishing Limited
Phoenix Mill · Thrupp · Stroud
Gloucestershire · GL5 2BU

First published 1998

Cover photographs: front: residents of Jervis
Street take part in a Public Gas Exercise;
back: Pte W. Buckingham VC. Page 1: Officers
and colours of the 3rd Leicestershire Regiment,
c. 1890.

British Library Cataloguing in Publication Data
A catalogue record for this book is available from the
British Library.

ISBN 0-7509-1809-8

Typeset in 10/12 Perpetua.
Typesetting and origination by
Sutton Publishing Limited.
Printed in Great Britain by
Ebenezer Baylis, Worcester.

To Jess, Samuel & Thomas

CONTENTS

Seven little monkeys. Men of the 11th (Pioneer) Battalion, Leicestershire Regiment, on the eve of their departure for France – 24 March 1916 – with their mascot, a monkey presented by Miss Flora Scott (see also page 55).

INTRODUCTION

T his book is about the impact that war has had upon Leicestershire and the experiences of Leicestershire people in war and preparing for war. It is not a military history of the county, nor is it a history of the county's regiments (though there is much to be learned of them). It is a study through historical photographs of Leicestershire at war.

Any photographic study of war will encounter a number of obstacles. Modern warfare – from the end of 1914 onwards – has been a secretive business. Unofficial cameras were not welcomed at the front and official ones were and are subject to censorship.

Secondly, many images from the second half of this century are still in private hands. They are still 'current' family photographs, cherished by individuals or families, and have yet to find their way into photographic archives.

There are gaps then in coverage – any collection will have strengths and weaknesses – and this book, drawn in the main from the photographic archive of the Leicestershire Museums, Arts & Records Service, reflects that. You will look in vain for photographs of the Royal Air Force. Leicestershire was the base for numerous squadrons but their activities were either unrecorded or the photographs recording them are still owned privately. The Royal and Merchant navies are under-represented too. Leicestershire men were at sea but their cameras, it seems, were not.

So, this is the story of a county at war told from one viewpoint. It is intended to be informative and entertaining. It is also a tribute to the servicemen and women, and their families, of Leicestershire over some 500 years. This book does not attempt to glorify war – 'War', in General Sherman's phrase, is 'all hell' – but it is a commemoration of self-sacrifice, fortitude and public spiritedness. It is also a story of great enjoyment, of 'seeing the world' and of the rewards to be had from doing a difficult job well. It is a record not only of preparing for and involvement in war but also of the effect of war on Leicestershire doorsteps.

The order of this book is therefore not chronological, nor by regiment or unit. It is rather by military experience – through enlistment, training, sport and mobilisation, to war and its aftermath. We begin, though, with a slice of history. . . .

The 1st Battalion, Leicestershire Regiment, at the King's Birthday Parade, Aldershot, 1912.

Part One: Army Life

CHAPTER ONE

1ST BATTALION, LEICESTERSHIRE REGIMENT

This chapter shows us an entire battalion, nearly 1,000 men, of the 1st Leicestershire Regiment on the eve of the First World War. We see not only the faces of every officer and man but also how they were divided, by company and by the functions they performed. These are the county's regular soldiers, who policed the empire, who made up the British Expeditionary Force in 1914, and who as a unit virtually ceased to exist after the first few months of 1915.

The battalion colours and drums. The regimental colour (a St George's cross because of the regiment's white facings) and drums bear the battle honours of the Leicesters from the Siege of Namur in 1695 to the Defence of Ladysmith in 1900–1. The Royal Tiger and 'Hindoostan' were awarded in 1822, after eighteen years' service in India.

The officers. In September 1912 the battalion left Aldershot for Ireland. The officers travelling with it were Lt. Col. H.L. Croker
Majs Dent and Dwyer; Capts Puckle, Gruchy, Everitt, Davies, Henderson and W.C. Dixon (the adjutant); Lts E.S.W. Tidswel
W.F. Planton, R.S. Dyer Bennet, G.C.I. Hervey, C.C. Rolph, H.S. Pinder, H.B. Brown and J.T. Waller; 2nd Lts J.W.E. Mosse
A. Weyman, W.H.G. Dods and J.C. Herring-Cooper; Lt. (and Quartermaster) J.H. Greasley and Bandmaster C.S. Witt

The sergeants 'are in command both within and outside the barracks of the sections of the company. . . . They a
responsible . . . for the armament, equipment, barrack utensils, &c. of the men, and also of the rooms inhabited. . . .
(Lt. Col. J.M. Grierson, *Scarlet into Khaki*, 1899)

The corporals – appointed by the commander of the battalion after an examination by the second in command, the adjutant and company commander as to their knowledge and suitability.

The battalion boys. The wing-pattern epaulettes, some decorated with drummer's tape, show that most boys were in the band. A limited number of youths of between fourteen and sixteen years of age were accepted into the army for training as buglers, drummers, artificers or artisans. Often such youthful recruits were the sons of non-commissioned officers of the regiment.

The band. The regimental march in 1912 was 'Romaika', an air inherited from the 64th Foot (it seems) in 1849, when the 64th's bandmaster, Wickels, transferred to the Leicesters. 'Romaika' fell out of favour, however, in the 1930s (the colonel in 1933 dismissing it as a Greek dance 'in which the dancers throw handkerchiefs at each other'). In that year the old militia quick march 'A Hunting Call' was adopted. The slow march 'General Monckton, 1762' remained.

The drums. From reveille to lights-out, the regimental day was punctuated and ordered by the battalion's buglers. The 'drums' had their own social life too, their teams often appearing in lists of sporting triumphs.

'A' Company, Capt. Everard F.S. Henderson's company. Henderson was killed, as a major serving with the 2nd Battalion, fighting the Turks at Shaikh Saad in December 1916.

'B' Company was commanded by Capt. Charles S. Davies, a New Zealander. From 1927 to 1931 Davies commanded the entire 1st Battalion. He was also the officer – seconded to the West African Rifles from 1907 to 1911 – who brought a company of West Africans to Britain for the Royal Tournament (see pages 36–7).

Capt. T.N. Puckle's 'C' Company. Puckle was an old soldier, having served with the battalion in South Africa (where he wa) twice mentioned in despatches) and throughout the Siege of Ladysmith. He did not accompany the battalion to France in 1914.

Capt. S.O. Everitt and the men of 'D' Company.

Maj. E.L. Challenor and 'E' Company. Challoner, later Lt. Col., CB, CMG, DSO, rose to command the battalion from August 1919 until 1923. Challoner's period of command saw the battalion engaged in police work in Liverpool and Ireland – prior to the creation of the Free State. His wife was even the victim of an IRA ambush at Athlone that left her wounded.

Maj. B.C. Dent's 'F' Company. Dent also rose to the command of a battalion of the regiment, the 2nd, and returned to visit his old comrades in 1941 as Brig. Gen. B.C. Dent CB, CMG, DSO.

Maj. B.C. Dwyer and 'G' Company. On 1 October 1913 the number of companies in an infantry battalion was reduced from eight to four, each new company doubling in size. Dwyer assumed command of his own and Capt. Puckle's company, to form the new 'C' Company.

'H' Company, Capt. F. Le M. Gruchy's. Gruchy was one of the first of the Leicestershire Regiment's officers to be killed in the First World War. He was killed in the last 'open' fighting of the war, before trench warfare became ubiquitous, in October 1914.

Lt. W.F. Panton with the battalion's machine-gun section. In 1912 the section consisted of Sgts H. Harris and S. Mastin, L. Cpl. J. Halford and Ptes W. Morton, S. Saunders, J. Setterfield, J. Bennett, J. Hawkes, P.R. Treherne, J. Ingram, G. Pallett, R. Madders, J. Pescord and H. Fletcher.

The battalion's signallers, with their signal flags (for semaphore) and begbie and limelight signal lamps. Only heliography is not represented, but as it depended upon the sun and the battalion was at Aldershot (rather than India for example), flags and lamps were more reliable. In good weather semaphore signals can be read up to 7 miles away and limelight lamps up to twice that distance.

The battalion scouts. In 1912 an infantry battalion such as the 1st Leicesters was provided with up to nine bicycles – for scouting, despatch-riding, and for the signallers to carry messages when all else failed!

Battalion transport: the transport sergeant and his carts. At its war establishment the battalion's transport would include one one-horsed cart, twelve two-horsed (including field kitchens), and three two-horsed wagons. They would carry medical supplies, tools and reserve ammunition. In addition, a 'baggage column' would supply one day's rations for all men and horses, spare boots and other necessaries, and carry the officers' baggage, battalion stationery and administrative papers.

CHAPTER TWO

EXERCISES, TRAINING & WAR

A small standing army recruited without conscription meant that for most Britons a century ago military experience was limited to either watching parades and listening to bands – or, more actively, joining the volunteers (or, after 1908, the Territorials). Volunteering meant occasional evenings of drill and a summer training camp.

The regular army trained too, of course, as small units or in 'manoeuvres' of whole brigades and divisions. In 1913 a full scale 'war' was fought across the Midlands as the army of Brownland fought the forces of Whiteland.

A photograph by the Leicester photographer G.M. Henton: he has caught the Coldstream Guards marching through Windsor in May 1894. The officer marching along the pavement is in his undress frock coat, while his men swinging along the road show very well the white serge shell jackets and highly polished brass buttons of undress drill order.

A picture full of movement, as the photographer has snapped the Leicestershire Militia executing a smart
left-wheel across Narborough Road, Leicester, one Sunday in 1890. Such a sight must have been a
powerful aid to recruitment.

...ifle volunteers at target practice, 1902. The photograph demonstrates the effect of black-powder — in this case fired ...om outdated Martini-Henry rifles. The result of thousands of troops all firing black-powder on the battlefield can ...adily be imagined.

...nd Lt. F.R. Griggs, under canvas with the Leicestershire ...olunteers, *c.* 1890. The choice of the Loughborough ...hotographer Robert Frost suggests a camp in ...harnwood Forest.

Officers of the Leicestershire Imperial Yeomanry (the 'Imperial' appeared during the South African War and survive until 1907) at one of its annual camps, *c.* 1905. Col. W.A. Peake DSO is nearest the camera and the stocky figure of Ma R.B. Muir, then commanding 'A' Squadron, is also shown.

Yeomanry Camp, *c.* 1905. The slouch hat worn by the fellow in the front row (the mallet-wielding one with t precarious seat) suggests a date shortly after the South African War. The annual training period had increased to compulsory minimum of fourteen days — but it was still fun! Even polishing boots, bridle and bit was fun: in god company, under canvas, in the open air, away from the family. . . .

ent *'avec beaucoup d'amour'* from the 1903 Leicestershire Imperial Yeomanry Camp near Melton Mowbray to Miss
Gwendolyn Warren, this postcard not only gave her an image of the Yeomanry — newly uniformed and equipped in the
light of the South African War — but tells us of the social side of camp life: 'we went to Belvoir on Sat. night, and are
going to Harby tonight. We go on our bicycles most evenings. . . .'

Territorials in camp, 1911. The camp of the 4th and 5th Leicestershire Regiments and associated Territorial units at
High Tor, Whitwick, in August 1911 provided a great opportunity for training and sport. Here a Lt. Williams (Lt.
. Williams, Lincolnshire & Leicestershire Brigade, Army Service Corps?) leads the way over the fences.

Home from home: a second lieutenant of the
1st Leicestershire Regiment showing off the
delights of tented life at Strensall Camp, near
York, in August 1912.

Leicesters (and friends), Aldershot, 1911.
The 1st Leicestershire Regiment's stay at
Aldershot (1910–12) was a brief one.
Training, inspection by King George V and
service at York during the rail strike seems
to have left barely enough time to button
up trousers for the photographer!

ampened ardour: the 3rd Battalion, Leicestershire Regiment, on parade at their summer camp, Edale, Derbyshire, July
)06. As the regimental magazine, *The Green Tiger*, recorded, the weather was far from ideal: 'If the rain was bad, the
ud was "worser", as we heard a Lutterworth lad remark. Such mud too! No respecter of persons! From commanding
ficers to drummer boys it welcomed them all! . . . A few days were spent in mountain climbing, with a field day on
rival at the top, but generally speaking, the regular training of the battalion was curtailed by the weather.' (*The Green
ger* II no. 9, page 9)

On manoeuvres: the 1st Battalion, Leicestershire Regiment, at rest prior to movement by train to Shorncliffe Camp, 1909. Their new webbing equipment (designed to be removed in one piece) scattered about them, the Leicesters relax or go with their mess tins for refreshment.

Territorials in camp, 1911. Charnwood Forest echoed with the tramping of ammunition boots and the crash of musketry in mock battle. The Lincolnshires camped at Garendon and the Leicestershires at High Tor Farm, Whitwick. The Leicestershires had been to High Tor twice before but 1911 was a vintage year. Five fields were taken and a huge encampment set up. The Army Service Corps took the left of the line, then the 4th Leicestershires. The 5th Leicestershires occupied the right of the line separated from the 4th Battalion by the officers' lines and – a novelty – huge mess tents (as above).

The 1st Leicestershire Regiment arriving at Lydd from Shorncliffe Camp, Kent, for firing exercises, 1909. 'Ern' wrote to 'Lizzie': 'This is part of our company marching into Lydd. I just managed to be taken. Roll on Tuesday. . . .'

Halt, 1911: Lt. Col. Croker confers with the officers of the 1st Battalion, Leicestershire Regiment. Usually a column on the march halted for the last ten minutes of every hour. As here, infantry would fall out to one side of the road and immediately remove their equipment. Fifteen miles a day was considered a satisfactory rate of progress.

1st Leicesters on the march, 1911. The British infantryman of 1911, fully equipped, carried more weight — up to 67 lb — than a medieval knight in armour. The weight, moreover, was mostly carried on the shoulders. So, it is small wonder if, after 10 miles or more, there ceased to be a comfortable way of carrying the 8 lb 10½ oz Short, Magazine, Lee-Enfield rifle.

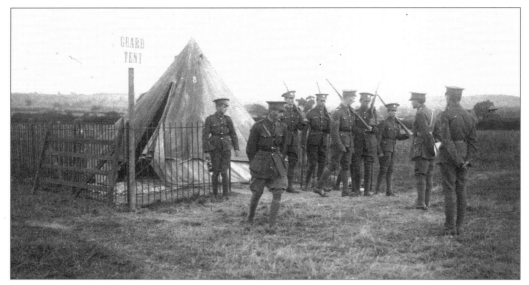

Eager to learn: the guard tent at the 1st Cadet Battalion, Leicestershire Regiment instructional camp. The camp was held at Burton Lazars from 29 July until 11 August 1916. No doubt things improved!

By the time this photograph of Thompson sub-machine gun practice in the Middle East was released, the Leicestershire Regiment had moved into Europe for the last stage of the Second World War. Here Capt. R.E. Langrish stands behind the machine-gunners, who include L. Cpls Skelton and Stobbs.

CHAPTER THREE

PARADES &
SPECIAL OCCASIONS

Ceremony has always played an important part in military life. It aids recruitment and it is a display of the power of the state. There is little doubt too that it always goes down well with the public. As this chapter will show, the elements of military ceremonial have varied little over the years. Indeed, it is probably this constancy and tradition that makes them so popular.

The Leicestershire Royal Horse Artillery fires its royal salute for the coronation of George V, 22 June 1911. The salute proved very popular, and led to speculation in the local press that perhaps this was the first artillery fire heard in Leicester since 1645 and the Parliamentarians' recapture of the town after Naseby!

Military review, 1869. The ten companies of the Leicestershire Militia are drawn up across Leicester's Market Place — mounted officers and the band to the side. The appeal of seeing friends, hearing the martial airs and the sight of a red-coated battalion was clearly a major attraction for mid-Victorian Leicester.

'Eyes Front'! The Leicestershire Yeomanry had earned the title 'Prince Albert's Own' after escorting
Queen Victoria and her Consort through Leicestershire in 1843. Here, on 29 May 1882, the Yeomanry in
full dress is again serving as an escort to royalty. En route to open Leicester's Abbey Park, their Royal
Highnesses the Prince and Princess of Wales paused in the Market Place to receive an address from Earl

Ferrers (as Provincial Grand Master of Freemasons). The Yeomanry served its purpose too, it being widely reported that one onlooker near Dover Street (either through intoxication or misplaced admiration for royalty) approached too close to the royal party in an effort to shake hands. Undeterred by a blow from the Princess's parasol, the over-familiar subject was seen off with the flat of a Yeomanry sword.

An officer and men of one of the two regiments of Life Guards, photographed by G.M. Henton, 27 May 1895.

Men of the Scots Guards, photographed by the Leicester water-colourist G.M. Henton, 5 September 1895. The troops are assembling outside the Guard Room in the Lower Ward, Windsor Castle. This excellent view of guardsmen in their marching order shows every angle of the slade-wallace pattern equipment.

Lt. Col. H.L. Croker, newly appointed to the command, at the head of the 1st Battalion, Leicestershire Regiment, at Aldershot, 1911.

The drums of the 1st Leicestershire Regiment lead the battalion through an admiring crowd at Aldershot, 1911.

The undoubted 'hit' of the 1908 Royal Naval and Military Tournament were the men of the West African Regimer
The detachment sent to the Tournament (seen here at the docks on arrival) was accompanied by its commanding office
Col. A.F. Montanaro, and Lt. C.S. Davies — seconded from the 1st Leicestershire Regiment. Davies is in uniform wi
the bowler-hatted and mackintoshed Montanaro.

En route for Waterloo! A flurry of papers –
presumably at Southampton – as Lt. C.S.
Davies assembles his detachment of the West
African Regiment on its way to the Royal
Tournament, 1908.

A corporal and two men of the West African
Regiment, *c.* 1908. This is a souvenir
postcard from the Royal Tournament,
where the regiment's mock jungle battle
(arranged by Lt. Davies of the 1st
Leicesters) proved the sensation of the show.

On 25 July 1919 Admiral of the Fleet Sir David Beatty travelled to Leicester from his hunting box at Brooksby to receive the freedom of the city. Appropriately he was met at the Great Central railway station by Leicester's Royal Navy and Royal Marine reservists.

The first duty of King George V on his arrival at Leicester for the royal visit of June 1919 was to inspect a guard of honour chosen from demobilised soldiers, all of whom qualified for the 1914 bronze medal. 'I think you have a very fine lot of fellows,' His Majesty told the organiser, Mr Pettifor, who is seen here behind the King.

Men of the Leicestershire Regiment assembled on Victoria Park for inspection by King George V. His Majesty had already been treated to an aerobatic display by the 'Leicester' aeroplane, a march past by Midlands battalions and a parade of 100 veterans of the first campaign of 1914. The opening shots of the First World War must have seemed a long time ago.

Mutatis Mutandis. . . . Another royal visit and another guard of honour. This time, Maj. F.M. Bishop escorts King George VI past the lines of the Leicestershire Regiment on 30 October 1946. A month later (on 28 November) the King's approval became clear – with the proclamation of the *Royal* Leicestershire Regiment.

Wooden rifles and flat caps: the Leicester Junior Training Corps on parade at the football ground, October 1914. Formed by Mr T. Crumbie, the former Hon. Secretary of the Leicester Rugby Football Club, the Corps trained nearly 7,000 youths too young for military service during the war. Crumbie's recruiting zeal did not cease with the Junior Corps; he was instrumental in raising the 11th Battalion of the Leicestershire Regiment – and nearly bankrupted himself in the process. It was Crumbie too who had printed the county's 'Roll of Honour', recording the names of over 9,000 Leicestershire men killed between 1914 and 1918.

The guard of honour on the occasion of King George V's visit to Leicester in June 1919 was drawn from the Territorial battalions of the Leicestershire Regiment. Lt. H.T. Grylls MC here carries the King's Colour past the YWCA on Regent Road, en route to the railway station.

The 'old' colours of the 2nd Battalion, Leicestershire Regiment, were laid up in the regimental chapel of Leicester Cathedral on 2 April 1927. The colours – seen here as they passed the London Road station – were carried by 2nd Lts Coburn and Beauchamp. The colours had been presented to the regiment at Lucknow, India, in 1885.

Capt. L. Sawyer DSO leads 'B' Company, 1st Battalion, Leicestershire Regiment, in the march past the Commander-in-Chief, Sir Robert Cassells (right, with stick), at Jubbulpore, India, 25 July 1936.

The Leicestershire Regiment was raised by Solomon Richards, who received a commission as colonel from King James II o 27 September 1688. Two hundred and fifty years later the 1st Battalion of that regiment (which had added 'Leicestershire to its title in 1782) was at Jubbulpore, India. The anniversary was commemorated in style and became a source of doubl celebrations with the presentation by Lord Linlithgow, the Viceroy of India, of new colours to the battalion.

CHAPTER FOUR

AT EASE

Here we see the army at ease. Off duty the soldier can be at his most relaxed or almost at his smartest – compare the Army Service Corps men lounging by their lorry on page 52 with the sergeants in the Channel Islands on page 45.

Spring cleaning in Magazine Square? An interesting view of the militia's headquarters in the late 1860s. Knapsacks, blankets, mess-tins (in their cases) and other items of clothing have been laid out on the barrack square. The brass plate on the door third from the left bears the legend 'PTACEK', and is presumably the accommodation of the Polish music professor Francis Ptacek, for many years bandmaster to the militia and a prominent figure in Leicester musical circles for nearly thirty years until his death in 1886.

The officers of the 17th Foot (the Leicestershire Regiment) assembled below the walls of their garrison. The 185
undress forage caps (with the 'Green Tiger' above the numeral '17') and the 1856 pattern single-breasted tunics worn b
the officers on the extreme right date this photograph to the late 1850s or early 1860s. It is most likely, therefore, tha
these are the walls either of Quebec or Halifax, Nova Scotia, the stations of the regiment from 1856 until 1865.

The tiger and battle-honours on the bass drum or the '17' on the officers' caps would each have identified this company a
coming from the Leicestershire Regiment. The figure in the centre in a blue cloth helmet confirms a date of between
1878 and perhaps 1880.

The bandmaster (centre) and two sergeants of the Leicestershire Regiment in walking-out dress, *c.* 1905. Despite the Royal Arms behind them, these soldiers have a distinctly 'Prussian' air, no doubt because of the Brodrick caps they wear. Named after the Secretary of State for War at the time of their introduction, William St John Brodrick, the caps proved intensely unpopular and lasted only until 1905 – slightly longer than Brodrick himself.

Above: Vital supplies, *c.* 1895. The proximity of the All Saints Brewery, Leicester, perhaps explains the high spirits of this detachment of the Leicestershire Yeomanry. The nature of the errand is not recorded, though the collection of sufficient drink for the annual training camp would at least explain the profusion of 'helpers'!

Left: A studio portrait of a youthful member of the Leicestershire Yeomanry, *c.* 1890. Although the Yeomanry proved itself ready and willing to serve when called upon to do so against the Boers in 1900, the social side of military life had always seemed paramount. The regiment's officers were the county's gentry and its men, 'reliable' yeoman farmers and their sons.

William Creagh and three fellow officers pose around a family album at Benares (now Varanasi), India, 1862. Creagh's album names them, left to right, as Creagh himself, Nelson, McGregor and Maitland.

A wedding photograph taken by R. Venkiah Bros of Sgt. Harry Lindley and his bride, Ann Hopewell. The ceremony took place at St Mary's Church, Fort St George, Madras, India, on 31 October 1904. Lindley had joined the 1st Leicesters as a boy soldier in the 1890s and rose to become a lieutenant and quartermaster.

Sgt. W. Reed and Cpl. Girling with some of
their comrades from the 1st or 2nd
Leicestershire Regiment. The good conduct
badges and wound stripes show the length of
service of these regulars. Possibly these are all
survivors of the First World War.

Leonard Evans (left) with two pals from the 8th
Battalion, Leicestershire Regiment. He was
born in Leicester and enlisted in Leicester but
was killed on 15 July 1916 near Mametz Wood.
In four days' fighting on the Somme, Evans'
battalion suffered no fewer than 432 casualties
– of whom 110 were killed, died of wounds or
went missing.

Gunners at Garendon Park, 1915: Lawrence Kellett, of Aylestone Road, Leicester, and his pals in 'D' Sub Section, 2/1 Leicestershire Royal Horse Artillery. He told his 'ma': 'I shall be home for the wk. end probably in a fortnight but I shall e pleased to see any one of you over a wk. on Sunday. The public are admitted 2 pm till 7 pm.'

The headquarters staff of the Leicestershire Yeomanry at Diss, soon after mobilisation, September 1914. It was while at Diss that the regiment – almost to a man – volunteered for service in any theatre of the war. By 3 November 1914 the Yeomanry were in France.

On 22 January 1918 the transports *Minnetonka* and *Mutlah* reached Suez and disembarked the 2nd Battalion, Leicestershire Regiment, fresh (though that is hardly the appropriate word) from the hard-fought Mesopotamian campaign. Until the end of March 1918 the

battalion remained at Ismalia, engaged in training and sight-seeing visits beyond the dreams of most Leicestershire men.

Above: Bert Ward of Dulverton Road, Leicester, with his pals (and a goat), fresh from basic training with the Army Service Corps, Grantham, 9 October 1915 (see also pages 53 and 58).

Left: Bert Ward in late 1918, now a motorcyclist in the Army Service Corps.

Bert Ward again, astride his motor bike, with two friends from the 239 Motor Transport Company, Army Service Corps, Peachey, November 1919. By the end of the First World War the ASC had increased from 6,500 officers and men in 1914 to over 330,000: more men than the regular British Army in 1914!

More Army Service Corps men with their Daimler wagon at Peachey, Bonfire Night, 1919. These men had waited nearly a year for demobilisation. Their lorry represents one of the great changes – to motor transport – wrought by the First World War. In 1914 the British Army had fewer than 1,000 lorries. By 1918 the Army Service Corps alone had 33,500!

Preparing 'scran', the cookhouse at Ripon, March 1916. 'Stewed beef, mutton or fowl. — Cut up the meat into thin slices or small pieces . . . put a little fat into the bottom of the cooking pot, and when hot put in the meat, stir till brown, add a sliced onion, carrot, or turnip, season with pepper and salt, add a little flour and some hot water, stir well, and allow to simmer slowly till done. Tomatoes, rice and powdered biscuit in lieu of flour may be added.' (*Field Service Pocket Book*, 1914)

Men of the 42nd Division Motor Transport Company, Army Service Corps, messing about in boats at Charleroi, Belgium, March 1919.

A youthful member of the Leicestershire Yeomanry, 1914. The 'Imperial Service Badge' worn above the right breast pocket signifies his readiness to serve overseas. The Leicestershire Yeomanry – with the other Yeomanry regiments – provided the cavalry arm of the Territorial Army, created in 1908 to ensure that any future British commitment to European war was a credible one.

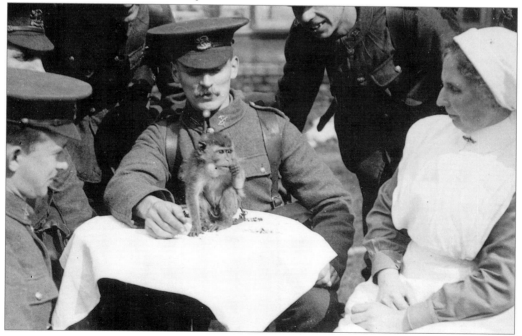

Pioneer monkey, 24 March 1916. The crossed pick and rifle on the collars of this monkey's friends identify them as men of the 11th (Pioneer) Battalion, Leicestershire Regiment. The photograph records Miss Flora Scott's gift to the battalion of a monkey mascot – on the eve of its departure for the Front. Miss Scott was well known as the proprietor of a nursing home in Victoria Road, Leicester.

Mosquito killers: Ptes Codd and Paling with their Indian assistants and 'weapons'. 'The "Rockfeller"
malaria film was sent to us recently, and all ranks of the [1st] Battalion enjoyed a free show of a highly
scientific film which depicted the invidious effects of malaria . . . a series of photographs of the Anopheles
mosquito from birth, through a short, gay life, to its end. . . .' (*The Green Tiger*, August 1929)

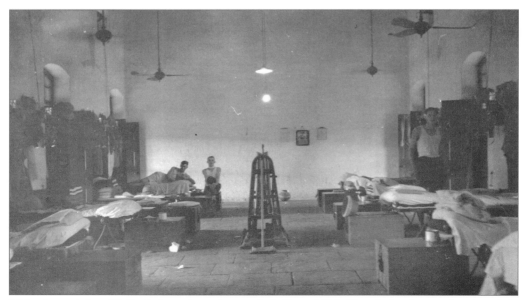

Little changed since Kipling's day: a barrack room in India, *c.* 1935. Electric fans have replaced punkahs
but there are few other amenities, and little else to do at the hottest part of the day but rest.

Above: Staff officers at the headquarters of the
Wana Column in Waziristan with soldier servant
and pet, *c*. 1919. The pet (of a Leicestershire
Regiment officer?) was doubtless as fierce as the
Waziris, and just as independent.

Right: Delilah's successors: men of the 2nd
Leicesters enduring a haircut in the Holy Land,
c. 1939. They were possibly the detached platoon
at Umm-al-Faraj (this roving unit was known
from its base as 'Fardet'), which was kept busy in
a constant guerrilla war with Arab rebels.

How many families, by the end of the First World War, possessed such a photograph – a studio portrait of a loved one in his first uniform? This is the portrait that Bertram T. Ward – the ASC man encountered already on pages 52 and 53 – sent home to Dulverton Road, Leicester.

CHAPTER FIVE

RECORDED FOR POSTERITY

The military man, it seems, has always been ready not only to serve his country but also to record that fact for posterity. From the earliest effigies of men-at-arms to the modern day, portraits of soldiers in uniform or groups of soldiers are the most readily found visual records of martial activity. What follows is a typical array. Few family albums will be without something of this sort.

The effigy of a thirteenth-century warrior at Tilton-on-the-Hill, attributed to Sir John de Digby who died in 1269. Digby (according to Nichols' History and Antiquities of Leicestershire) *served both Edward I and II in their Scottish wars.*

The figure of George Manners, the fourth son of John, Earl of Rutland, on the monument to his parents at Bottesford. Although Elizabethan sculptors (in this case Garret Johnson of Southwark) often adopted considerable licence in depicting men in armour they never owned – let alone wore – Manners saw active service in Ireland against the Earl of Tyrone's rebels. He was knighted there by the Earl of Essex, apparently for valour, though enemies at court were quick to denounce Essex's generosity with honours among his friends.

The monument erected by Frances, the widow of Sir William Noel, Bart, at Kirkby Mallory has almost certainly the last effigy of an amoured man-at-arms in a Leicestershire church. The armour is that of a cuirassier, a heavy cavalryman, known – for obvious reasons – as a 'lobster'. The use of such armour here tells us more about Sir William's social status than his military experience or prowess. He died in 1675 aged thirty-three and his widow had the monument put up 'In Honour of his Memory . . . when she had been almost 4 yeares a Widdow'.

Capt. Henry Holland, 1800. The threat of invasion by Revolutionary France led not only to the formation of the Leicestershire Yeomanry but also a crop of volunteer infantry units. Among them was Capt. Holland's Loyal and Independent Loughborough Volunteer Infantry. Raised in August 1794, the company remained in arms until 1808 when it disbanded and 150 men transferred to the Militia.

George Anthony Legh Keck, of Stoughton Grange, who led the Leicestershire Yeomanry as its lieutenant colonel commandant from 1803 until his death in 1860. Although liked and respected by his corps, it was the admiration by amateurs for an amateur. Keck's professional military experience was brief in the extreme and his reliance on a capable adjutant and regimental sergeant major absolute.

An Army doctor in 'mufti'. In 1891 William C. Creagh was living at Grangewood Lodge, Netherseal, and working as a GP registrar from a surgery next door. The son of a lieutenant general and brother of a colonel, Creagh himself rose to the rank of surgeon major in the Army Medical Department. His scrapbook-cum-photograph album is a marvellous source of military photographs from the 1860s and '70s.

From William Creagh's photograph album, the non-commissioned officers of 'H' Battery, 'F' Brigade, Royal Horse Artillery, 1864. Taken in India, this photograph illustrates well how little allowance was made for the hotter climate. The quartermaster sergeant leaning to the right of the 6 pounder's muzzle shows a fine array of medals. The third is for service in the Indian Mutiny; the others are less clear (perhaps the Crimea?).

Another photograph from the Creagh album, *c.* 1870. This shows the renowned one-armed general Sir Samuel Browne (whose sword-belt, designed to overcome the disadvantages of having lost his left arm, is still one of the distinguishing marks of an officer in armies throughout the world) with his staff. The bearded officer is John Creagh, Browne's assistant quartermaster general.

Another photograph from Creagh's album, this one showing him (standing, rear) with fellow staff officers at Jellalabad, Afghanistan, 1879. Reclining on the charpoy is Purdy, while Hepbourne and Walsh are seated. The other standing officer is not named, though he is identified as a veterinary surgeon.

Above: The Roman III prominently displayed here on the regimental colour tells us that these are the colours and officers of the 3rd Battalion, Leicestershire Regiment – the old Leicestershire Militia. The uniforms are those of the 1890s.

Left: A well-equipped cavalryman, photographed by C.W. Cooper of 20 Beatrice Road, Newfoundpool, Leicester. His bandolier of ammunition is of a type superseded in 1903 and the sword belt worn under the tunic suggests a light cavalry unit – but beyond that his identity and regiment are a mystery. It seems likely, though, that our trooper – a hussar, lancer or light dragoon – is off to fight the Boers, and the date is 1899 or 1900.

A Leicestershire Imperial Yeomanry trooper ready – from the crown of his slouch hat to the bottom of his stohwasser gaiters – to fight the Boers on the veldt, c. 1902. The British Army had learnt a hard lesson in the Transvaal and Orange Free State. Our trooper has a more practical hat, carries his ammunition in a bandolier rather than awkward pouches, and has a rifle (not carbine) slung ready for use.

More lessons from the Boers: warrant officers and sergeants of the Leicestershire Regiment wearing the slouch hats a
bandolier equipment introduced after the South African War. The bandoliers lasted from 1903 until the appearance
webbing in 1908.

The occasion of this parade in the Market Place, Loughborough, *c.* 1912, is not recorded. It may simply be the assembly
of one of the Territorial Army battalions of the Leicestershire Regiment preparatory to its summer camp – perhaps
Whitwick or Garendon.

The bandmaster and drummers of the 3rd Battalion, Leicestershire Regiment — the old Leicestershire Militia, *c.* 1910. The side drums bear the badge of the regiment and its twelve battle-honours. By 1918 that number had nearly doubled.

The drums of the 11th Battalion, Leicestershire Regiment, the 'Midland Pioneers', *c.* 1915.

A private in 'undress', photographed at Belgaum, India, c. 1906. Both regular battalions of the Leicestershire Regiment were in Belgaum for three days in October 1906 as the 2nd Battalion arrived to relieve the 1st.

Capt. Geoffrey Codrington (seated, centre) with the officers and non-commissioned officers of 'A' Squadron of the Leicestershire Yeomanry, c. 1913. The faces and demeanour of these men – as much as their trade and efficiency badges – show the confident ease of the Yeomanry on the eve of the First World War.

269 Pte. Albert Henry Locke with chums from the 6th Battalion, Leicestershire Regiment, *c*. 1916. Locke and his
ends wear the 'emergency' leather equipment issued in 1915 owing to shortages of webbing. Sadly Locke did not live
see the Armistice: he died of wounds the day before, on 10 November 1918.

. Col. E.C. Atkins and the adjutant, Capt. R.P. Shea, with the warrant officers and sergeants of the 2/5th Battalion,
icestershire Regiment, at Stockwood Park, Luton, 26 July 1915.

Officers of the 2nd Battalion, Leicestershire Regiment, recently arrived in France from India, January 1915. Three faces do not fit: Brig. Gen. C.G. Blackader DSO (Commander of the Garhawal Brigade, of which the Leicesters were part) and two interpreters, Monsieur St Andre (of the Chasseurs Alpine?) on the far left and 2nd Lt. Morgan, far right.

Officers at the headquarters of the 1st Leicestershire Regiment near Bethune, France, 1917: Maj. J.W.E. Mosse (?) with officers of his battalion, two visitors from the 9th Suffolks, a machine-gunner, a staff captain and the medical officer.

Douglas Hackett and his comrades of the 176th (Leicester) Howitzer Brigade, Royal Field Artillery, somewhere in France, *c.* 1916. This photograph was sent home to his parents at Exton Road, Leicester. Like all but half a dozen of his fellow gunners, Hackett survived the war.

Machine-gunners of the 10th Battalion, Leicestershire Regiment, with their instructors from the Yorkshire Regiment and their weapons: a Lewis and a Vickers machine gun. Each was theoretically capable of firing 500 or more rounds a minute. Two such guns were considered adequate for a battalion in 1914, even excessive by some. By 1918 each battalion had thirty-six Lewis guns and access to a divisional reserve of sixty-four Vickers. War had become slaughter.

Above: The commander of the Wana Column and his staff after the successful recapture of Fort Wana during the 3rd Afghan War of 1919. The column commander, Reginald Dyer, is now far better known for his mishandling of civil disorder in the Punjab – leading to the Amritsar Massacre – than for his capable conduct of the Wana campaign.

Left: Pte. Albert Bunce, in India, *c.* 1930. The regimental flash (red and white with a thin black stripe down the middle) on his Wolseley helmet puggaree tells us that he is of the Leicestershire Regiment. Doubtless the silver top to his privately bought swagger-stick bears the regiment's badge.

company of Leicestershire Territorials outside the Army recruiting office possibly in Melton Mowbray, *c.* 1935. It is
kely to be 'B' Company – the Melton, Harborough and Oakham Company – of the 5th Battalion. The men are proudly
nowing off the German Efficiency Shield.

n the spring of 1939 the expansion of the Territorial Army led to the splitting of the old 5th Battalion, Leicestershire
Regiment, into 1/5th and 2/5th Battalions. This is 'B' Company of the 1/5th at Melton Mowbray, the sprinkling of battle
ress among the old service dress perhaps indicating the new 'expansion' intake.

Market Harborough Battalion, Leicestershire Home Guard, October 1944. Back row, left to right: CSM J. Harri Lt. S.A. Clarke, Lt. G.M. Goad, Lt. P.V. Davies, Lt. W.E. Stokes, Lt. A. Baillie, RSM W. Nixon, CSM J. Walley. Fro row: Maj. S.P. Stoker MC, Capt. W.R. Vince MC, Maj. E.G. Gillian DSO, Lt. Col. H.D. Belgrave DSO, Cap R.F. Pickering, Capt. W.H. Simpson, Capt. J. Hobbs.

The Band of the 7th Leicestershire Home Guard, c. 1944. Back row, left to right: B. Pollard, T. Leeds, C. Buswel J. Bird, S. Allbright, L. Orringe, R. Mattock, W. Draper, E. Brown. Front row: S. Nunn, W. Brown, F. Allbright E. Pollard, J. Hobbs, L. Mason, E. Pollard, L. Perry, J. Almey, A. Orringe.

he sergeants (above) and officers and men (below) of the 15th Battalion, Parachute Regiment, at Melton Mowbray, June 1944.

Maj. W. Richey, the chief instructor (seated, centre) and Cpl. J.R. Kettle (rear, left) of the Royal Army Veterinary Corps
with graduates of the Army Equitation Course at the RAVC Training Centre and Depot, Melton Mowbray, *c.* 1960. Th
Royal Marines officer seated to Richey's right perhaps confounds the old joke about 'horse-marines'!

CHAPTER SIX

SPORTS

The shape of trophy and the length of shorts may change but besides that, photographs of military sportsmen vary remarkably little. This chapter is therefore misleadingly slight. Sporting photographs, especially of team groups, abound, their profusion reflecting the great significance of sport in all the armed services from the mid-nineteenth century onwards.

Maj. B.C. Dwyer (centre) with his bayonet fighters, 1912. 'There are many people who, when talking about modern warfare, say that the day of the bayonet has passed — that the terrific fire of magazine rifles and Maxim guns will prevent any troops approaching close enough to each other to come to actual hand-to-hand fighting with the bayonet. You must not entirely believe this.' (Sir F.G. Guggisberg, Modern Warfare, *1903)*

The 1st Battalion, Leicestershire Regiment, boxing and gymnastic class, at Fort St George, Madras, India, 1903. At the centre sits Lt. Col. J.G.L. Burnett, with the adjutant, Bt. Maj. A.H. Wilkinson, to his right and Sgt. Maj. A. Wood to his left. Above (in bowler hat) is Pte. A. Conway with his companion clown, Pte. B. Jackson. Seated at the front are the boxing-gloved Ball brothers, B. and P.

For many peacetime soldiers before the First World War (and doubtless since) sport was their principal activity. The pages of the regimental magazine *The Green Tiger* are filled with news of sporting triumphs at rugby, soccer, hockey, swimming, shooting (of course), cricket, boxing and weight-lifting. This is the athletics team, the winners of the General Lawson Cup, *c.* 1912.

The 'real' Tigers: the 1st Battalion, Leicestershire Regiment, rugby football team, winners of the Army Cup in 1908, 1911 and the probable year of this photograph, 1912.

The 1st Battalion, Leicestershire Regiment, association football team, *c.* 1912. The Army Six-a-Side Competition bowl and Aldershot Senior Cup are a sign of their ability and success.

Officers of 'H' Battery, 'F' Brigade, Royal Horse Artillery, India, 1864. Comrades of W.C. Creagh (see page 62), the surgeon, jotted down their names: Ewbank, Bailey, D. Pemberton, C.H. Barnes and R. Mantill.

Part Two: War

CHAPTER SEVEN

ENLISTMENT

The First World War changed everything. No longer was war a distant thing read about in the morning papers. Every family was involved. Britain's army expanded in a few short months from a few hundred thousand to several million. When the flood of volunteers slowed, conscription renewed its force. These photographs, though, are all from that early period of the First World War, when enthusiastic crowds flocked to the colours with little notion of what might befall them.

Newly attested volunteers, almost certainly in the first few days after the declaration of war in August 1914.

The Town Hall recruiting office, Leicester, 1915 – readily accessible to any Leicester man who saw the stern visage and pointing finger of Earl Kitchener on Leete's famous recruiting poster and felt that its message applied to him. In all, Kitchener's appeal for recruits raised thirty-six divisions – ready and eager for battle by mid-1916 and the Somme offensive.

New recruits assembled in Magazine Square, Leicester, August 1914. The magazine and its associated buildings served as the headquarters firstly of the Militia and later of the 1st Volunteer Battalion, Leicestershire Regiment. The Militia houses were finally demolished in 1967 and their space occupied by De Montfort University.

A new recruit writes home, 1914: 'Dear Ethel, Can you find anyone you know on this? Puzzle find me. Have not come home this week because of upsetting mother and Grandma. Had quite enough last week on the Monday morning. Have you been over to Rothley yet? I expected a letter on Friday but was disappointed. Please write back always by return mail or I shan't write. If you have written since I shan't get your letter until Tuesday now. I am going to Old Wigston today & tomorrow to see some old school chums, boy & girls, but don't get anxious. Will write and let you know all about it dear. All my love, ever your own, George. Put No. 11616 C coy on either not 4th Coy.'

'Dear Ethel, This was taken just as I came from having a bath not bad considering the circumstances. We expect moving to Sanhurst [sic] Training College some time this week so don't write till you hear from me again. Love George.' This photograph shows George and his pals at Ripon shortly after his selection for officer training, late in 1914.

New recruits from 'Kitchener's Army' in the blue uniforms issued because of shortages of khaki, learning to march in step, late in 1914. The leader of the nearest column, George Griffin Ward Sleath, progressed through Sandhurst and training in Ireland to an eventual rank of major and, in October 1918, a Military Cross.

CHAPTER EIGHT

TO THE FRONT

Until the Zeppelin brought the front line to us in 1915, war had been (since the Jacobites turned for home at the Leicestershire border at least) a geographically remote experience. Trains and troopships were a vital part of war and even in modern war — from the great mobilisation of 1914 — it was the railway and the troopship that carried away our troops. The photographer was there too, of course, whether it was the Yeomanry in Melton Mowbray, the Artillery at Knighton Junction or the Leicesters aboard ship at Southampton.

Her Majesty's Indian Troopship Crocodile, *c. 1875. This was one of many troopships that brought fresh troops out to garrison the empire and carried the time-expired home. The Grand Hotel de France beside the bows of the* Crocodile *suggests a brief stop at Port Said or Suez, perhaps, after having negotiated the recently opened Suez Canal en route from India.*

'. . . arriving at Southampton about noon, we steamed on into the sheds where we left the train falling in with our kit
facing the vessel Guelph very soon we formed a line passing our rifles, kit bags helmets etc. onto the ship. . . . we
returned on board to have our Photos took by Mr Seville of Leicester all the company being collected at the stern after
that we had a look round the ship which was very large & every thing in the best order & beautifully clean at last the order
was given all aboard & at 3.15 pm we were towed out into the Solent where the Tug was cast off & we commenced our
long journey.' Pte. Frank R. Rippon, Service Company, 1st Volunteer Battalion, Leicestershire Regiment, en route for
the South African War, 1900.

The deck of a troopship – the SS
Mongolian – bringing the men of the 7th
(Leicestershire) Company, Imperial
Yeomanry, (and others) home from
South Africa, 1901. The voyage took a
month from Cape Town to 'Blighty'.

Leicestershire Regiment territorials mobilised and awaiting instructions, *c.* August 1914.

The Leicestershire Yeomanry, probably 'A' Squadron, at Melton Mowbray or Oakham, mobilise, August 1914.

The newly mobilised Leicestershire Royal Horse Artillery halted on the south curve leading into Knighton Junction, August 1914: an ideal opportunity for friends and family to say goodbye to artillerymen off to join the British Expeditionary Force. The Midland Railway trucks, loaded with field guns, limbers and wagons, can clearly be seen behind the carriages.

Capt. Geoffrey Codrington at the head of 'A' Squadron, Leicestershire Yeomanry, shortly after mobilisation in August 1914. The squadrons mobilised at their respective headquarters, 'A' at Melton, 'B' in Leicester, 'C' at Loughborough and 'D' at Lutterworth – though 'D' Squadron was later distributed among the others. The regiment moved to Grantham by mid-August and then, with the rest of the North Midland Mounted Brigade, went to Diss in Norfolk and from there to join the BEF in France.

Capt. Codrington improves his 'seat' as the Yeomanry pass down Gallowtree Gate, Leicester, August 1914.

More of the Leicestershire Yeomanry pass through Melton Mowbray, past the Old Bishop Blaze in Sherrard Street, August 1914.

A view from behind the Yeomanry column soon after mobilisation in 1914. By February 1915 the unlikeliness of an end to trench warfare and shortages of infantry led to the Yeomanry's going into the trenches near Ypres. A second line unit was raised and by 1916 was based on the East Coast against the possibility of invasion.

The departure of a company of Leicestershire territorials and a parting kiss outside the London Road station, *c.* 1914. The use of out-dated equipment (leather ammunition pouches rather than the 1908 webbing) suggests a date early in the war.

A draft of the 10th (Reserve) Battalion, Leicestershire Regiment, is seen off at the London Road station by relatives and the band from the depot at Glen Parva, *c*. 1916.

CHAPTER NINE

ON ACTIVE SERVICE

These are probably the rarest photographs of all. Few Victorian photographers could have captured 'action' before the advent of celluloid film in the late 1880s. Battle scenes survive as 'art', of course, and battlefields — after the event — have always been a popular subject. The Box Brownie camera brought the South African War before us — just as censorship (and a ban of private cameras) took the First World War away as a subject. There are snapshots here of both world wars and of 'peacetime' soldiering in India, Palestine and Ireland.

An evocative photograph of British infantrymen on the march, c. 1914. The clogging of roads by troops and wagons was a common sight on both sides of the English Channel in August and September 1914.

The Yorkist dynasty came to an abrupt end on Bosworth Field on 22 August 1485, with the defeat and death of Richard III. These stalwarts re-enacted the battle for the great Pageant of Leicester City and County in June 1932.

'In warres he spent his youth. . . .' These words are from the monument at Quorn to John Farnham Esquire, who died in 1587 aged over eighty. Sadly the monument – which depicts a siege of the mid-sixteenth century in great detail – is silent about the precise nature and scenes of Farnham's military experience. His later years were spent at court as a gentleman pensioner of Queen Elizabeth I.

Safely emplaced behind their entrenchments and earth-filled gabions, a pair of heavy guns — culverins or cannon — bombard the walls and towers of a continental town. The alabaster of John Farnham's monument shows superbly the detail of this Elizabethan siege battery.

Waiting to storm the breach made by John Farnham's siege guns, the 'forlorn hope' (from the Dutch 'verloren hoop', meaning 'lost troop') huddle together behind an entrenchment. The helmets and corselets of these pikemen show that they are heavy assault troops, companions of Farnham's perhaps from his warlike youth.

On 6 September 1642 Prince Rupert – camped at Queniborough – wrote to Leicester's mayor to request a 'loan' of £2,000 for the war chest of Charles I. Rupert's PS made clear his frame of mind: 'If . . . you shall refuse . . . I shall to Morrow appeare before your towne . . . with horse, foote, and cannon as shall make you knowe tis more safe to obey than resist his Majesties Commands'! Rupert was offered (and accepted) £500. This is the Prince as seen in the 1932 Pageant.

These top-hatted Victorian gentlemen are exploring the scene of the main Royalist attack on Leicester in 1645. The Newarke wall – the Civil War gun-ports still visible here – was stoutly defended, but after a day's bombardment and assault was overrun and the town sacked.

Labelled 'Ulundi battlefield' by Surgeon Maj. Creagh (see page 62) – but is it? The Arab boy and the earthworks suggest Egypt or the Sudan. Is it perhaps one of the Egyptian batteries at Tel-el-Kebir, spectacularly captured after a night assault by Sir Garnet Wolseley's expeditionary force in 1882?

A general view of Ladysmith, Natal, South Africa, *c.* 1902. For 121 days, until 28 February 1900, the 1st Battalion, Leicestershire Regiment, was besieged in the town, short of food and under bombardment from Boer guns on the hills around the town. For the last month of the siege 'chevril', or horse soup, was the staple of the daily ration: little wonder that 400 of the battalion's 1,000 officers and men were in hospital by the time the relief column arrived. (Photograph courtesy of R.E.J. Boyle)

Withdrawal to Ladysmith, October 1899. The opening shots of the South Africa War were fired just befo
6 a.m. on 20 October 1899. A British force, including the 1st Battalion, Leicestershire Regiment, h
encountered the Boers entrenched at Talana Hill. Outmanoeuvred, and with their commander mortal
wounded, the British fell back on Ladysmith. Here the Leicestershire's Mounted Infantry Company rid
despondently back from Talana in torrential rain. Before them were the 121 days of the famous siege.

Lt. the Hon. P.C. Evans-Freke, possibly mounted on the pony he bought at Gouda, South Africa, on 20 March 1900. Freke, with a company drawn from the Leicestershire Yeomanry, volunteered for service against the Boers – reaching Cape Town in March 1900. (Photograph courtesy of R.E.J. Boyle)

A Vickers-Maxim 1 pounder in action with the Leicestershire Yeomanry. Though made in Britain, these guns – soon to be known (after their characteristic noise) as 'pom poms' – were bought by the Boer Republics. The British Army had to learn their value the hard way before putting in their own order! (Photograph courtesy of R.E.J. Boyle)

P.C. Evans-Freke (pipe), Sgt. Maj. Ewart (field-glasses) and two Yeomanry officers take cover near Tiger's Kloof, Orange Free State. Four columns, including that of the Yeomanry, had converged on Christiaan de Wet's Boers. Then, on Christmas Day 1901, de Wet turned the tables on his pursuers, catching a Maj. Williams and his Yeomanry column unawares at Groenkop. The result was yet another British disaster — and the escape of de Wet. (Photograph courtesy of R.E.J. Boyle)

War on the South African veldt was a disheartening and exhausting affair. A fast-moving Boer commando, the quarry of pursuing British columns, was often glimpsed far in the distance. Only artillery had the range to inflict damage at such times: here Leicestershire Yeomanry examine Boer wagons wrecked by shells. (Photograph courtesy of R.E.J. Boyle)

These photographs of 'D' troop, Leicestershire Imperial Yeomanry, watering its horses and crossing a drift, or ford, in South Africa, show clearly the conditions typical of the latter stages of the second Boer War. Men and horses rapidly became worn out to little effect as British columns criss-crossed the veldt chasing their enemies' dust. (Photographs courtesy of R.E.J. Boyle)

Crossing Scherwispont Drift, 1901. Attached to Sir Leslie Rundle's division, the Yeomanry wearily pursued de Wet's Boers. Progress was slow and Rundle was soon transformed in his soldiers' minds to 'Leisurely Trundle'. Evans-Freke rather scathingly termed a day's inadequate progress as 'Rundled' or 'Much Rundling'. As these views of river-crossing demonstrate, however, Rundle had much to cope with. (Photograph courtesy of R.E.J. Boyle)

Rafting a 15 pounder across Delang's Drift, c. 1901. (Photograph courtesy of R.E.J. Boyle)

Lt. Hardwicke with the Yeomanry column's 'pom pom' in South Africa, *c.* 1901. The belt that fed the 1 lb shells – like a machine-gun → into the Vickers-Maxim can be seen beside its 'off-side' wheel. Each shell burst into fifteen fragments and they continued to be fired as long as the trigger was depressed. (Photograph courtesy of R.E.J. Boyle)

WAR! Such at least was the headline in the *Leicester Daily Post* of 18 August 1911. A combination of excessively high temperatures and employers' intransigence had led to a summer of industrial unrest. Coalmines, shipyards, docks and railways all saw trouble. In Leicester the storm broke just before the August Bank Holiday when the Amalgamated Society of Railway Servants called out their members and effectively closed both the Midland and Great Central Railways.

Railway guards. The government response to the railway strike was swift. By the evening of 18 August 600 men of the Queen's (Royal West Surrey) Regiment had been sent to the depot at Glen Parva by special train. The next evening a 'special' was again used to take troops into the London Road station, to secure the station itself, the engine sheds and signal boxes.

The Queen's Regiment came fully prepared, in full marching order, with ball cartridges issued. Signallers occupied the signal boxes and observant journalists noted the presence of stretcher bearers. Oddly, the blue Home Service helmets were worn, and their similarity to police helmets accidentally emphasised the military role as support for the civilian police. By 21 August the dispute was over and the troops withdrawn. The four days had afforded the Queen's Regiment some fun, but cost the Great Central over £26,000 and the Midland £54,000.

Capt. J. Bacchus (right) commanding 'C'
company, 1st Leicesters, with Lt. H.B. Brown, in
France, September 1914. Bacchus was wounded
in October 1914 and finished the war as the
officer commanding the depot at Glen Parva.
Lt. Brown rose, by 1917, to command the
battalion, earning the DSO en route.

A private of the 177th Infantry Brigade (the 2/4th
and 2/5th Battalions of both the Lincolnshire and
Leicestershire Regiments) at Luton, where the
brigade was in billets between January and July
1915. His leather equipment (webbing had been the
rule since 1908) and Japanese rifle testify to the
stretched nature of Britain's military resources.

Countess Markievicz, a prisoner after the
Easter Rising in Dublin, 'snapped by the
padré'. The 2/4th and 2/5th Leicesters were
both despatched to Ireland as soon as news of
the Rising broke. With the Countess may be
James Mallin, who commanded the rebel
outpost in Dublin's St Stephen's Green.

The expectation of the 2/4th and 2/5th Leicesters that they would soon be sent to France or Flanders was
confounded at Easter 1916 by the Rising in Dublin. Crossing from Liverpool to Kingstown on 27–8 April,
they found themselves behind makeshift barricades, defending Kingstown and Ballsbridge from the rebels.
'Houses searched, arrests made. Some sniping during evening and night' records the 2/5th Battalion *War
Diary* on 1 May 1916. On 10 May a mixed column of Royal Field Artillery, Royal Irish Horse and one
company of the 2/5th was despatched towards Tralee – where this photograph was taken.

Two photographs, taken by an observer from the 1st Leicestershire Regiment (?), of the Black Watch – with their distinc red hackles – engaged in 'police' work during civil disturbances in Bombay in 1929.

A sangar, or hill-top entrenchment, permanently occupied by one officer and twelve men (with a mountain-gun in support) as an outpost of Fort Wana, in Waziristan on the North West Frontier of India: this type of defensive position was well known to generations of soldiers of the Leicestershire Regiment.

Machine-gunners, India, *c.* 1935. Although unidentified, this photograph shows what is probably part of 'D' Company – the Machine Gun Company – of the 1st Leicesters, at the 'Machine Gun Concentration' held at Kohat (for competition and training) in 1934. The range-takers, with their instruments, lie between the two Vickers guns.

A snapshot of Indian troops road-building on the North West Frontier in the 1930s. A picket on the highest crags keeps careful watch for hostile movement.

Lorried infantry, North West Frontier of India: 'a bit rough going, its as bad as being on a ship. How would Dad like to drive one of these? Note the length of Bonnett [sic.] 92.5 hp'.

Looking almost more like brigands than regular soldiers, these men of the 2nd Leicesters were busy waging war on 'Oozles' – or Arab insurgents – in Palestine, from 1938 until 1940. Responsible for keeping the peace in the Acre Sub-District, the undermanned battalion was constantly on the alert for sniping rebels, road blocks and ambushes.

An escort for the Mukhtar – or village headman – at Bala, Palestine, *c.* 1939. The photograph illustrates well the relaxed attitude to dress regulations in the 2nd Leicesters.

Men of the 2nd Battalion, Leicestershire Regiment, acting in aid of the Civil Power, Bombay, 1946. As independence loomed closer, discontent grew in India. In February 1946 four companies of the Leicesters were called out to keep the peace in Bombay, threatened by mutineers from the Royal Indian Navy. There was more rioting in September 1946 that continued on and off until the end of the year.

CHAPTER TEN

CASUALTIES

War is not a safe profession. Even without the activities of an enemy, soldiering could be unhealthy. Dirt, disease, and inadequate or unsafe food and drink have all combined in the past to kill or injure many more soldiers than bullets or bayonets ever did, thus these photographs of the military hospital and military funeral are more than relevant. The role locally of the 5th Northern General Military Hospital from 1914 to 1919 has earned it a sub-section of its own.

Surgeon Maj. Creagh's photograph of the Officers' Quarters at Netley Hospital, just outside Southampton, c. 1870. In Creagh's day the status, morale and consequently recruitment of Army doctors was at a low ebb. The Officers' Quarters must have echoed in their emptiness. Now divided into flats, the building above, the hospital chapel and the mental patients' block (now occupied by Hampshire Police) are all that remain of the huge Royal Victoria Hospital, until the 1960s said to be the longest single building in Europe!

A snapshot of life (and death) aboard a troopship: the sale of the personal property of a Staffordshire Imperial Yeomanry sergeant who was buried at sea. This scene was photographed by the Hon. P.C. Evans-Freke, of Glaston, Rutland, who served with the Leicestershire Imperial Yeomanry in South Africa in 1900. (Photograph courtesy of R.E.J. Boyle)

Members of the Voluntary Aid Detachments Corps unloading wounded soldiers at the Midland Railway station, Leicester, c. 1917. No fewer than 363 such ambulance trains were met at Leicester by the VAD, and a total of 56,250 wounded were carefully unloaded and transported to the Base Hospital.

This sadly typical view of Leicester's Granby Street in 1918 shows an artilleryman, on leave with his family, and three convalescent servicemen in their 'hospital blues' — the hospital uniform of blue flannel jacket and trousers, white shirt and red tie, topped with the patient's own uniform cap or bonnet.

A Royal Flying Corps funeral, c. 1916 — perhaps one of the 500 or so wartime deaths at the 5th Northern General Hospital, Leicester.

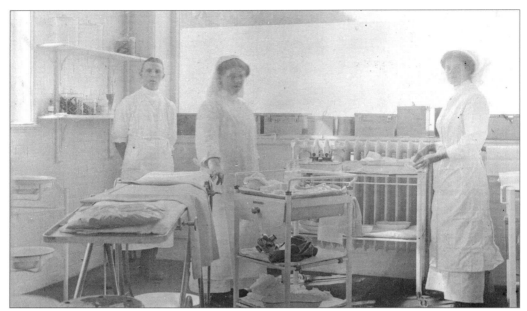

One of the results of the 1908 Army reforms, which created the Territorial Forces, was the establishment of the 5th Northern General Hospital. Originally with no premises and a staff of forty-six, on mobilisation the hospital moved into the old county mental hospital on Victoria Road, Leicester (now one of the university buildings), and expanded – eventually – to a staff of over 400.

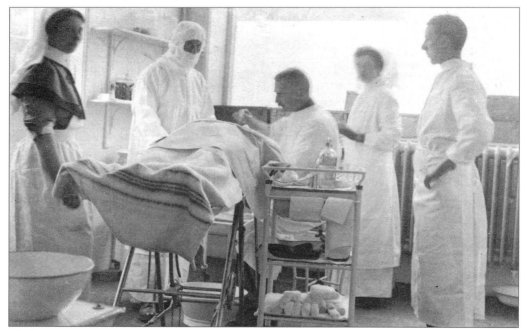

The first patient was received on 1 September 1914. By the departure of the last, on 10 September 1919, the hospital had dealt with 74,652 patients – including 59 prisoners of war. The operating rooms saw some 7,800 operations, with more at the North Evington Poor Law Infirmary once it was adopted – on 6 April 1915 – as a war hospital.

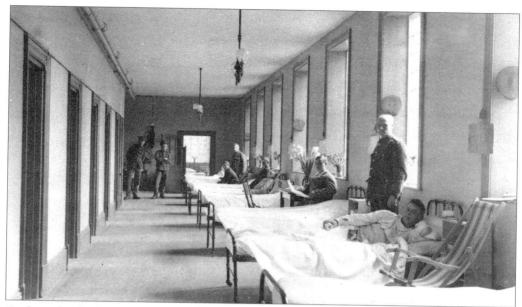

On the outbreak of war the Hospital Unit was in training at Netley (see page 113). Within a day, however, Col. A.V. Clarke had received the old mental hospital from the Leicestershire and Rutland County Councils and was touring the empty building with the architect S. Perkins Pick, planning the wards and offices.

In addition to whist and other card games, patients were kept entertained indoors and out. Each ward was equipped with a piano, a billiard table and a gramophone. Outside, the walking wounded could play cricket, tennis, bowls, croquet or clock-golf. There was a football pitch too but generally it was used by the staff. Outside exercise was not dependent upon good weather either – the grounds were well provided with shelters, and a covered skittle alley was available.

The gates to the 5th Northern General Hospital. No fewer than 425 convoys of wounded were received through the gates between September 1914 and June 1919.

Capt. W.M. Holmes of the Royal Army Medical Corps (officer commanding the North Evington War Hospital) with three patients and an RAMC sentry. This view, taken by Maj. Rothsay Stewart, looks surprisingly similar today.

Medical staff of the 5th Northern General Hospital. Back row, left to right: Capt. W.M. Holmes, Capt. E.L. Lilley, Capt. R.R. Young, Capt. F.B. Carter, Capt. W.I. Cumberlidge, -?-, -?-. Front row: Maj. H.J. Blakesley, Lt. Col. R.W. Henry, Col. L.K. Harrison, Lt. Col. R. Pratt, Maj. R. Sevestre.

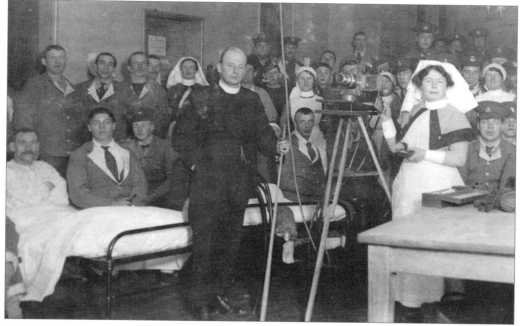

At least twenty chaplains were appointed to the hospital during the war, often for only a few months. The parson here – ably assisted by matron – is likely to be a civilian visitor. How entertaining his lantern slides were is open to conjecture, however – or perhaps the flash of the camera made a surprisingly large number of wounded soldiers blink!

The Sergeants' Mess. The Royal Army Medical Corps staff at the hospital gradually rose in number until 271 other ranks were working or being trained on the site. The increasing use of female nurses, supplemented by VADs, gradually reduced that figure.

'Men going off' is the original title of this scene. During its operation the hospital returned 54,111 men to duty, discharged 4,157 permanently unfit, transferred 12,000 to other hospitals, demobilised 3,870 and lost 514 who died from wounds.

'Smudger's Funeral 1931' is the only comment made on this photograph. The entire 1st Battalion, Leicestershire Regiment, then stationed at Ambala, India, is seen as the road winds behind the coffin.

The funeral of six men of the 1st Leicesters, killed at Hilversum, 10 May 1945. The battalion was engaged in the disarming of German troops in Holland – including some of the enemy's hardest cases from a Dutch German SS division. By some accounts (though the regimental history is silent) suicidal Germans unable to accept defeat deliberately detonated the dump of discarded arms – killing thirteen Leicesters (seven bodies were 'missing') and wounding six others: a tragic end to a tragic war.

The grave of Pte. E.G. Squires of the 1st Leicestershire Regiment, who died of dysentery at Kuala Lumpur on 28 July 1942 while a prisoner of the Japanese.

CHAPTER ELEVEN

PRISONERS OF WAR

Leicestershire soldiers have, presumably, been taken prisoner by their enemies since the Middle Ages and before. The county has also played host to prisoners. Many Yorkists were held after Bosworth in 1485 and Ashby-de-la-Zouch became a fairly 'open' prison for officers of Napoleon's army. In the First World War Donington Park did service and in the latter part of the Second the Leicestershire countryside fairly swarmed with Italians helping on the land and with Germans behind barbed wire or working on road schemes.

Food parcels, 1915: collecting for Leicestershire men held prisoner in Germany. The stall, beneath the South African War memorial in the Market Place, Leicester, shows the variety of goods sought. Largely through the efforts of the Rev. Francis Payne, vicar of St Margaret's and chaplain at the gaol, Leicestershire's POWs were comparatively well off: by 1917 each prisoner was sent three 10 lb parcels every fortnight by the combined POW Committee of the Leicestershire Regiment and Leicester churches.

Donington Hall in its First World War guise as a camp for German officer prisoners of war. The Gothic hall and chapel, designed by William Wilkins in the 1790s, are obscured by wooden huts, and Humphrey Repton's landscaped parkland is cut across by barbed wire fences and watch towers.

Although the popular impression in Britain, that the prisoners at Donington Park lived a life of well-fed comfort and ease, was strenuously denied by both Gunther Plüschow and Erick von Rintelen who wrote of their time there, it is clear that the commandant, Lt. Col. F.S. Picot, did his best for his prisoners. Hockey and tennis were played by the Germans, lectures arranged and great freedom granted to wander around the Park during the day. Only at night were the prisoners confined behind the barbed wire and electrified fences of the inner enclosure.

New arrivals for the prisoner of war camp at Donington Park. 'Outside the station we were greeted by a howling mob, comprised of women and under-sized lads and children, but few men. . . . The women and girls, belonging to the lower classes, behaved like savages. Yelling and whistling, they ran alongside and behind us, and occasionally a stone or a lump of dirt hurtled through the air.' (G. Plüschow, *My Escape from Donington Hall*, 1922; see also pages 124, 126 and 127.)

A sentry in the watchtower at Donington Park.

The elderly soldiers of the Leicestershire Regiment, armed with their elderly rifles, on guard at Donington Park. 'I made friends with a nice old English soldier, whom I presented occasionally with a few cigars, and invited to a glass of beer in the canteen.' (Gunther Plüschow)

Kapitänleutnant Gunther Plüschow of the Imperial German Navy's flying service. Narrowly escaping capture by the Japanese when they seized the German colony of Kiao Chow in China, Plüschow fled to the USA. Returning to Europe on an Italian steamer, he was intercepted at Gibraltar. After a brief stay at a camp near Dorchester, Plüschow was moved, in May 1915, to Donington Park.

'A mixture of vaseline, bootblack and coal dust turned my blond hair black and greasy; my hands soon looked as if they had never made acquaintance with water; and at last I wallowed in a coal heap until I turned into a perfect prototype of the dock labourer on strike. . . .' (Gunther Plüschow) Having slipped over the 9 ft barbed wire fence at Donington Park, Plüschow sped to London by train from Derby via Leicester. From there a Dutch steamer carried him to Flushing, home, and an Iron Cross of the first class.

The 1/5th Leicestershire Regiment was the first unit from the county to see action in the Second World War. Despatched to Norway at a time when Oslo and Trondheim were already in enemy hands, the battalion arrived divided in half and without any vehicles (which sank with the transport *Cedarbank*). Despite remarkable tenacity and courage, the result was inevitable. Some of the Leicesters escaped to neutral Sweden, others were picked up by the Royal Navy, while the rest (like Sgt. Freakley shown here) began a lengthy captivity as prisoners of war.

A snapshot of Italian prisoners of war (of whom only 'Bruno' – of the white braces – is identified) helping with the potato harvest in north-west Leicestershire, *c.* 1943.

For them the war was over. German prisoners of war are marched through Leicester, possibly after Victory in Europe, May 1945. Many prisoners worked for years before repatriation, working on farms or civil engineering schemes.

Troops of the 1st Battalion (originally raised as the 8th but renumbered after the capture of almost the entire 1st Battal
by the Japanese) accepting the surrender of German forces, at Hilversum, Holland, May 1945. The tragic outcome of t
last episode of the war may be seen on page 121.

C H A P T E R   T W E L V E

THE HOME FRONT

This is a title that properly belongs to the world wars of this century. From 1914 onwards war has involved the whole country, with a complete mobilisation of manpower and production for the single aim of winning the war. Enemy action has brought the home into the firing line too, with the threat and actuality of aerial bombardment, and the Civil Defence intended to cope with it.

The United Nations Parade held in Victoria Park, Leicester, on Sunday 14 June 1942. Leicester's Lord Mayor, Miss Frisby, accompanied by the Bishop of Leicester, Capt. Fouquies of the Free French, the Chief Constable and Brig. W.D. Wellman of the Salvation Army (among others) took the salute as representative units of the Army, Civil Defence, cadets and other youth organisations marched past — in honour of the twenty-eight nations united against the Axis powers.

Although from 1903 the British Army had had a Motor Reserve, it was – bizarrely – disbanded in November 1913. The offer from Leicestershire motorists on the outbreak of the First World War to form a Leicester Motor Corps was therefore eagerly accepted. At first largely a flying column of armed motor-cyclists (led in this instance by Cecil Bray, of the Leicester solicitors Bray & Bray, in his two-seater fawn Stellite), the Corps did sterling work later in the war ferrying wounded troops from the railway stations to hospital. The presence of only one uniformed Corps member – in a jacket of lancer style known unkindly as a 'maternity jacket' – suggests a date early in the war, probably *c.* 1915.

The YMCA Association Hall, East Street, Leicester. Now the venue for comic opera and film shows, in 1917 the YMCA (or 'Y Emma' to the signallers of the First World War) provided basic accommodation for troops on leave or in transit. In this case the 'young men' include Australians and a Scotsman.

No. 6725 Buckingham, Pte. W., VC. In spring 1916 William Buckingham returned to the Cottage Homes at Countesthorpe (where he had lived from 1892 to 1901) to visit staff and meet the residents. A year before, at Neuve Chapelle, he had won the Victoria Cross for persistent acts of bravery over two days – crawling out into no-man's land to rescue wounded men. A modest man, Buckingham did not relish his notoriety and preferred a return to active service to helping recruitment and training. He was killed on the Somme on 15 September 1916.

Robert Gee was born in Metcalf Street, Leicester, orphaned soon after and admitted to the Countesthorpe Cottage Homes. Like William Buckingham, Gee joined the Army, rising to the rank of quartermaster sergeant by the outbreak of the First World War. In 1915 he was commissioned and at Cambrai in 1917 he won the Victoria Cross – after escaping from German captivity and (though wounded) capturing an enemy machine gun. In 1924 Gee was elected MP for the Bosworth Division. He died in Australia, aged eighty-three, in 1960.

A Short 184 seaplane, fitted with bombing equipment, at Fishguard, 1918. One of a batch of thirty planes ordered fr◌
the Brush Works in Loughborough, this aircraft gained notoriety when, on 22 March 1918, it managed to bom◌
German 'U' boat off Fishguard.

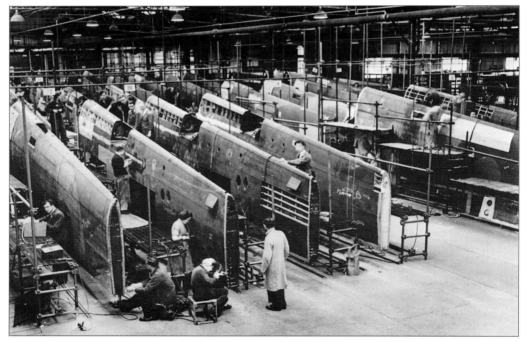

Lancaster wings, c. 1944. This is the mainplane repair shop at the Brush Works in Loughborough. Parts
salvaged from crashed aircraft were repaired (Brush's role was to renovate the wings), reassembled and
the rebuilt Lancaster bombers returned to active service.

A 'pom pom' gun produced by the British
United Shoe Machinery Company, *c*. 1916.
With its high-angle fire mounting and sight, this
'pom pom' demonstrates one of the horrific
developments of warfare in the twentieth
century: aerial attack. It seems unlikely that
such comparatively primitive weapons posed
much of a threat to enemy airships or
aeroplanes, though the resounding 'pom, pom,
pom, pom' must have cheered the crew of any
ship or anti-aircraft fortification under attack.

Guarding the Bofors gun: workmen with an anti-aircraft gun at Melton Mowbray, *c*. 1945.

Cut-throat at work, *c.* 1916. Although it is not an easy task to identify a tartan from a black and white photograph, it seems likely that the victim (or perhaps beneficiary?) of manpower shortages on the Home Front is a Seaforth Highlander.

Blanche E. Harrison, conductress no. 666 for Leicester Transport throughout the Second World War. She represents another aspect of twentieth-century war – the 'mobilisation' of the entire population, if only to carry on the vital work left undone by men called to the colours.

Women's Day, 17 April 1918: a parade through Leicester to enhance recruitment for the Land Army, Voluntary Aid Detachment and Women's Auxiliary Army Corps. 'The Women Land Workers (numbering about 100) in their sensible and becoming costumes carried the implements of their calling and were followed by wagons drawn by splendid horses, and the girls from an instructional factory bore sections of aeroplane wings, symbolic of their calling. . . .' (*Leicester Daily Post*, 19 April 1918)

A practical lesson in Midlands agriculture: Leicester Melbourne Road School girls potato-picking in north-west Leicestershire, *c.* 1943–4.

The threat of enemy attack seemed to come a step closer with the sandbagging of public buildings in 1939. The thickness of sand needed as protection against bomb-blast is evident in front of the city police station in Charles Street, Leicester. The mild curiosity of passers-by is captured well here – as is the mixture of council and police labour.

In the autumn of 1939, with Air Raid Precautions planning well under way in Leicester, it was decided that the provision of shelters at the Mantle Road School was inadequate. As an exercise in practical education – as well as to avoid calling upon scarce manpower – it was decided that the senior boys would build their own air raid shelters.

Team leaders were chosen, and learnt from their schoolmasters the secret of a good mortar and how to lay English bond brickwork.

The four Mantle Road shelters were each 43 ft long by 9 ft wide and 6 ft 9 in high. The walls were 14 in thick, sitting on a 4 in thick bed of concrete. The roof, of reinforced concrete, was between 8 and 9 in thick, enough to survive all but a direct hit.

Mr F. Gentle supervises the footings of the front wall. As the school's own account states: 'The boys entered into the scheme with the greatest enthusiasm, and were rightly proud of being the first elementary school to be entrusted with such work.'

'The roof called for careful thought and preparation as a deadweight of over twenty tons had to be supported. An elaborate system of wooden props, bearers, and shuttering was erected to support the concrete on the inside, while other timbering was necessary on the outside . . . to form the overhang, the edge, and the drip-channel.'

'Nothing but a National Emergency could have caused the class room work to be thus superseded. . . . The value of the practical experience . . . is self evident but besides this, the boys saw that foresight, carefulness, steady hard work, and self discipline, were necessary for the common good. . . . They took on an exacting task, and proved themselves capable of bringing it to a successful conclusion.'

The Mantle Road School shelter's 'foundation stone', incised by Roy Hill and laid by the chief bricklayer, K. Barker.

The value of neighbourly co-operation in wartime is obvious. Neighbours' Leagues therefore prospered as streets or districts united for fire-watching and other ARP duties. Here a Mr Thacker issues stirrup-pumps – first line of defence against incendiary bombs – to his neighbours, *c.* 1940.

Getting to grips with their new gasmasks, volunteers for Leicester's Air Raid Precautions learn the vital importance of a tight fit, 25 January 1938.

The appearance of the Luftwaffe in the skies above Leicestershire — the first bombs on the county fell between Dunton Bassett and Ullesthorpe at about 1 a.m. on 25 June 1940 — brought home the reality of Total War. Here the residents of Jervis Street in Leicester demonstrate, in a Public Gas Exercise, their acceptance of steel helmets and gasmasks in everyday life.

On 28 January 1938 Leicester held a rehearsal for its air raid black-out. Corporation staff practised dealing with liquefied gas: this pair carried the solution used to neutralise the liquid. 'I've worn the mask for half an hour,' one man told the *Evening Mail*, 'and it would not be much discomfort to wear it for the limit of two hours. You get a bit warm, that's all.'

Though gas was never used, the threat remained throughout the Second World War. Exercises were regularly carried out involving both first aid and gas decontamination. Here, wounded are dealt with at the official opening of new ARP depots at Western Park and Rowley Fields in Leicester, 2 May 1942.

A carnival atmosphere is in evidence at this Civil Defence display in Leicester, 5 August 1942. Summer weather no doubt made the mobile gas cleansing unit's demonstration more appealing than it might have been for the 'bathers' in February!

By the time of this practice evacuation of wounded by ARP workers in April 1942, the worst of the raids were over and plenty of real experience lay behind the drills.

Word reached Loughborough shortly before 7 p.m. on the evening of Monday 31 January 1916 that Zeppelins were on their way. Besides an ineffectual black-out there was nothing to do but await their arrival. The huge, slow airships were high enough to defy most fighter aircraft and Loughborough was undefended by anti-aircraft guns. The first bomb fell in The Rushes, killing a woman and smashing windows and roof-slates.

Another fell in Empress Road (seen here) and two more in the main street and in a nearby garden. The Zeppelin had passed in under five minutes, but left six women and four men dead and a dozen more injured. To the German High Command the Zeppelins (and airships produced to other designs) were too much effort for too little result. To the people of Loughborough they were a sign of Total War.

A lone German aircraft, presumably lost, dropped the first bombs to fall on Leicester at 10.15 a.m. on 21 August 1940. They fell across Cavendish Road, killing six and injuring twenty-four people. The gas main was also fractured, and was still alight when this photograph was taken.

The worst raid on Leicester, however, was on the night of 19 November 1940, the same week as the devastating attack on Coventry. The Highfields district suffered worst, though several Leicester landmarks – Faire Bros' premises in Rutland Street, T. Grieve & Co.'s in Southampton Street and Arthur Kemp's Dover Street Works – were all gutted by fire. The destruction can be gauged from this view of Highfield Street and Severn Street. The wrecked vehicle is a trailer ambulance, blown across the road.

Perhaps to accompany the major Air Raid Precautions display at the Home Life Exhibition held at the Granby Halls, Leicester, the city held another major ARP exercise in September 1938. The John Bull Rubber Company's decontamination squad were on parade – and eagerly photographed for the local papers.

C H A P T E R T H I R T E E N

VICTORY PARADES

A homecoming and a cause for celebration. The great national efforts of this century and the privations and losses associated with them have occasioned huge demonstrations of pride and rejoicing. Leicester's celebrations after the First World War were capped by the visit of the King and the grant of city status.

Veterans of fighting at Laing's Nek and Belfast, the officers and men of the Service Company, 1st (Volunteer Battalion) Leicestershire Regiment, receive a warm welcome from comrades and the people of Wigston Magna, as they march through the town en route for the depot at Glen Parva, 23 May 1901.
(See page 86 for their departure.)

On 15 November 1918 the Duke of Rutland presided over the presentation of 121 gallantry medals to soldiers of many units, discharged soldiers and to the families of deceased servicemen. Col. Westmacott called out the names and, amid roars of approval, the recipients stepped forward for their Military Medals or Distinguished Conduct Medals.

The Naval detachment marching at ease towards Leicester's Victoria Park for its review by King George V. The march past was the highlight of a royal visit that included a twenty-one gun salute by four anti-aircraft guns specially brought to Leicester for the occasion, and called at Corah's factory and the museum on New Walk to see a stuffed royal tiger that the King had himself shot in India.

Victory in Europe. A Sherman, followed by a Churchill tank, trundles past 'Top-hat terrace', down the London Road into Leicester, 1945.

Victory Parade in Leicester's London Road, 1945. Representative units of the fighting services, Civil Defence and police, fire and ambulance services parade through the city.

CHAPTER FOURTEEN

REMEMBERING THE DEAD

The survival of the annual commemoration of the dead of the First and Second World Wars, though in some ways a shadow of what it once was, demonstrates the depth of national loss felt in 1918. Earlier, that sense of grief was no less but was concentrated in fewer families. We see both responses here – though the individual monuments below are inevitably of the wealthy classes.

It is fitting that a study of war should conclude with remembrance of the dead.

Naval trophies at Kirkby Mallory. Capt. Thomas Noel RN, commander of His Majesty's ship Princess Louisa, *was killed in an engagement with the French off Minorca on 20 May 1756. Though buried in the English church at Gibraltar, Noel's family erected this tribute to him and decorated it with emblems of his profession.*

The monument at Stanford-on-Avon to Capt. Edmund Verney Wyatt-Edgell, one of only two British officers killed at Ulundi – the last battle of the Zulu War of 1879. The sculpture, signed by Felix Joubert, depicts Wyatt-Edgell in profile on an obelisk while an officer in the full dress of his regiment, the 17th Lancers, places a wreath beside it. Pieces of Wyatt-Edgell's uniform and equipment may still be seen at Stanford Hall.

More details from the monument to Capt. Wyatt-Edgell, including his gauntlets and lance-cap beside a Zulu shield and a pair of throwing spears ('izijula'). Ironically Wyatt-Edgell was not speared but shot through the head. His regiment was released from the British Square at the end of the battle to complete the rout of the Zulus and to round up prisoners; it was Wyatt-Edgell's misfortune to come across a strong, well-armed party of warriors who rose in ambush from long grass as he led his lancers across a donga (or dried river bed).

When the armoured cruiser *Hampshire* struck a mine and sank in June 1916, she took with her to the bottom not only two sailors and two Royal Marines from Leicestershire but also Horatio Herbert, Earl Kitchener. The fact that Kitchener's father had lived at Cossington made the Earl, to many, a local man too. The memorial service and procession from the Town Hall to St Martin's, Leicester, attracted a considerable crowd. Here is the detachment of Royal Marines and sailors, followed by walking wounded from the military hospital.

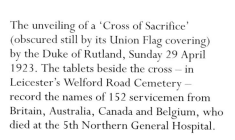

The unveiling of a 'Cross of Sacrifice' (obscured still by its Union Flag covering) by the Duke of Rutland, Sunday 29 April 1923. The tablets beside the cross – in Leicester's Welford Road Cemetery – record the names of 152 servicemen from Britain, Australia, Canada and Belgium, who died at the 5th Northern General Hospital.

The vast Arch of Remembrance in Leicester's Victoria Park was unveiled on Sunday 5 July 1925. Despite the presence of the Bishop of Peterborough, the architect Sir Edwin Lutyens, the Mayor of Leicester and other dignitaries, the unveiling was performed by an old lady, Mrs Elizabeth Ann Butler, who had had three sons killed in France, another dead of consumption caused by active service and two others wounded. The arch unveiled, the buglers then sounded the Last Post and Reveille.

A trophy of war, c. 1920: a captured German fieldgun, probably the Rheinmetall 7.7 cm Fieldgun 16, on display outside the Castle in Leicester. The First World War had been fought on the Home Front too, so it seemed right that civilians should receive their share of the 'spoil'.

'We shall remember them': Armistice Day, Tuesday 11 November 1924. Crowds await eleven o'clock in Town Hall Square, Leicester. Behind them is the temporary war memorial that recorded how few local families escaped the First World War unscathed. Only the need for full production in the Second World War could have justified the movement of commemoration from Armistice Day itself to Remembrance Sunday – thereby avoiding costly stoppages of machinery and traffic.

Territorials of the Leicestershire Yeomanry and Leicestershire Regiment at a parade – perhaps for Armistice Day – at Melton Mowbray, c. 1925.

A couple of German soldiers fly home from the war, *c.* 1914 – but how did this postcard reach Leicestershire? From a prisoner of war at Donington Park perhaps? Or loot brought back from the Western Front?

ACKNOWLEDGEMENTS

The photographs in this book have been drawn principally from the collections of the Leicestershire Museums, Arts & Records Service, stored at the Leicestershire Record Office in Wigston Magna. Some contemporary photographs are from the author's own collection and others are used with the permission of Mr R.E.J. Boyle, of Bisbrooke, Rutland.

Thanks are due to the Leicestershire County Council photographer, Roger Vaughan, for his meticulous work. Especial gratitude must go to Kim Goodwin whose patience, accuracy in typing and ability to read scribble never cease to astound.

Most of all, though, I must thank my wife for her advice and encouragement – without which I would still be pondering over the contents page.

BRITAIN IN OLD PHOTOGRAPHS

SUTTON'S PHOTOGRAPHIC HISTORY OF TRANSPORT

To order any of these titles please telephone our distributor, Littlehampton Book Services on 01903 828800
For a catalogue of these and our other titles please ring Emma Leitch on 01453 731114